101 Treasurable Poems of Body, Soul, & Spirit

Written By: Chad Joseph Thieman

Author, Publisher, & Designer: Chad Joseph Thieman

Editors: Tina Bryant & Debbi Moore

Cover Photos: Kirsten Thieman
Photographed: Trenton Thieman
Author Photo: Tina Bryant

Permission Is Granted:

May the Spirit of the LORD shine forth

through all who believe...

..manifesting the Kingdom of Christ

to all the world!

~ Chad

This book is dedicated to my parents

A Special Thanks ~

I am most thankful for the Father and Son; and their shared Spirit of Righteousness, who now resides within me. I am thankful for my physical birth, but even more grateful for my spiritual manifested birth. In the Father, I am made alive through the inner workings of His Spirit, and through the rising of the Sun of Righteousness within me.

I would like to extend personal thanks to my family. You truly have helped me become who I am today. It is through my deep inner love for you that I have found such great encouragement to continue my writing.

Thank you to all those who have supported my dream. You mean more to me than you will ever know. You have not only participated in the fulfillment of my dream, but you have likewise participated in the fulfillment of the Father's dream. I will always remember your loving kindness; as well as, the value you represent as a true friend.

May the Father's Spirit enter within, and may His Sun of Righteousness arise in your hearts.

Blessings, Chad

Malachi 4:2

A Table of Contents

*** *Bonus Short Stories*

Foreword

I met Chad many years ago, when I worked with him in Lenoir, NC. I was one of the door greeters at a department store, and he was a young stockman. It seemed that Chad always had something special about him, like a glow around him. He really cared for people and always had such a big heart. One time when I was feeling down, he bought me an angel. It was these early years that helped shape Chad into the man he is today, a man who loves God and loves life. Chad can write a poem that can fill your eyes with tears. His writings come straight from the heart. He writes about love and about God. He is a great inspiration to me. He is one of the angels that walk among us. Chad you are my angel. I am so glad God put you in my life. I love you and I look forward to seeing you in Heaven. Goodbye my angel. Love, Mary

*** Mary Bryant passed away shortly after writing this. Her life was a beacon of light to many, through her own writings of inspiration, and the positive spirit she displayed toward others. I am grateful to have had her as a friend. Before she passed, I had asked her to write one last poem that would inspire the world. Her poem "Stars" is featured in the bonus poetry section at the back of this book. Within one week from handing me the poem, she was carried off by the angels. Mary's life was a testimony of Christ, and his Kingdom through and through, and she lived out that legacy until the very end. I hope you appreciate her poem "Stars", as much as I do!

Introduction

The book <u>101 Treasurable Poems of Body, Soul, and Spirit</u>, is the third installment of Chad's treasurable and poetic anthology. Book three completes his original trilogy. This volume carries with it the heart of <u>Faith, Hope, and Love</u>, (the first in the series), and the passion of <u>Life, Love, and Light</u>, (book two). You will experience genuine romance, spiritual works pertaining to the Christian faith, and poems of nature's ambient sanctuaries. Each collection includes a title page with a prayer and a Bible verse; as well as, several poems dealing with the overall subject. The book includes 101 categorized poems, each of which has a reference to Scripture. Also included are a couple of short stories found throughout the work; several proverbs by the author; and a few bonus poetry sections in the back of the book, which includes fifteen additional poems. This treasury of poetic verse is sure to satisfy any avid poetry lover.

The Adventure of Life Collection

Walk this journey with me daily LORD, that I may not have to walk it alone!

Psalms 139:23-24

Along the Appalachian Trail ~

A brisk Appalachian breeze,
Brings the scent of fresh fallen leaves;
As they lie upon the path,
The path of uncertainty.

And, I'm standing here once again,
With my face against the wind;
Reflecting on who I am,
And the places I have been.

Finally seeing beyond the regret,
I know, I must never forget;
All that brought me to this place,
Upon the mountain of God's grace.

I pause to take it all in,
The air, the view, the Spirit's wind.
Along this trail I find serenity,
As His presence and grace envelop me.

Psalm 16:11

Signs of Life ~

As you wander upon this earth,
God's Spirit will be your guide;
Showing you in sight and word,
As He opens up your eyes.
All around you are signs of life,
Leading you along the way;
And helping you be ever wise,
As you go about your day.
You may see them right off hand,
And know their meaning too;
Or it may take a second glance,
And a prayer to see the truth.
God's Spirit will reveal things,
Which few ever knew;
Secret things He put in place,
Will help awaken you!

Proverbs 16:9

Standing At the Crossroads ~

I stand at the crossroads of life,
Attempting to walk two paths.
My flesh longs for all the world has to offer,
To experience the greatest of pleasure;
While the spirit within seeks to inspire,
By leaving a lasting legacy behind.
I know that these two roads,
Can never be as one;
I must choose which path to walk upon.
Do I live for the Spirit in eternal realms,
Or satisfy the flesh where pleasure abounds?
I stand here at the crossroads of life,
Knowing the way in which I must go;
A path with its share of troubles and strife,
With blessings above and crosses below.
I surrender my wants of this earthly realm,
To walk that road which is Heaven bound.

Psalm 23:3

The Journey of Life ~

You come to a divide in the road,
Along the journey of life;
Wondering which way you should go,
In a world of chaos and strife.
It's time to make your choice,
Between the paths which lie ahead;
Just listen to that one, still voice,
Guiding your journey ahead.
Before you, the road divides;
But on which will life be found?
The road filled with earthly pleasure,
Or the one of heavenly crowns?
Will you choose the way of pride,
Or deny yourself, and let the Lord guide?
The choice my friend, is up to you.
So which is the road you will choose,
Along the journey of life?

Acts 9:1-6

You'll Never Walk Alone ~

A Father once told his Son --

"Son, you'll never walk alone;
Even though you venture out,
Far away from home.
For deep within your heart you'll find,
Reason for life's song and rhyme.
My love you hold inside you,
Will help to always guide you;
Through good and troublesome days,
As you learn to walk in my ways."

The Son replied --

"Father, I know you will not leave me,
Until I reach my journey's end.
I know you'll go with me,
As I teach and heal each man.
Within my heart I'll always carry you,
Over land and over sea;
Until the moment of atonement,
Upon Calvary's lonely tree.
It is through my blood,
That many sins will be atoned;
So that others will hear the words,
You'll never walk alone."

Matthew 28:18-20

The Inspire Love Collection

Inspire me LORD, that I may go forth in Your Spirit and inspire the nations!

1 Corinthians 13:4-7

Inspire Love ~

When the days are dark and lonely,
And darkness seems your only friend;
When the news is always negative,
And the heartaches seem to never end...
..It is at these times, God calls us,
When all the world seems wrong;
To see beyond the raging storms,
To a sea that's still and calm.
At these times, He gently whispers,
"You are made for so much more."
He beckons us to step out in faith,
And walk through heaven's door.
To that place of higher perception,
Where believers can see far above;
A world that is filled with sorrow,
And begin to inspire love.

Hebrews 10:23-24

Inspire Love Packages ~

Giving an Inspire Love Package,
Can bring a smile to any face.
A basket full of thoughtful gifts,
Can ease a burdensome weight;
A fresh baked loaf of homemade bread,
A mug with scented coffee grounds,
A decorative pillow for a weary head,
And an album of inspirational nature sounds.
Make a commitment to give one each year;
Whether it's to a friend or a complete stranger.
Your love package, they'll forever hold dear.

Include a giftbook to encourage their faith,
A message of love, and something of sweet taste.
Take one to a child in their hospital bed,
Or a homeless man on the street;
Inspire a lonely soul in prison,
Or anyone you see with a need.
Send one with a letter of forgiveness,
Or ask for forgiveness yourself.
Every soul has need of inspiration and love,
And you may be the vessel to help.
For what good is humanity,
Without the Spirit from above;
Or with no one being moved,
To go forth and inspire love?

Luke 6:38

May We Seek the Heart of God ~

May we seek the heart of God;
Above all else in our lives.

May we receive the Spirit of God,
And have Him be our guide.

May we know the mind of God,
And do all that is good.

May we listen to the voice of God,
Until He is understood.

May we obey the Word of God,
Always following in His way.

May we shine forth the light of God,
And turn this darkness into day.

Acts 13:22

The Poet of Light ~

The poet of light,
Is the poet in Christ.
There is no greater desire,
Than sharing the Gospel
With elegant fire.
Reproving all those
Destined to be saved,
And raising them up
From shadowy graves;
To eternally dwell
In the Father's light;
A timeless mouthpiece,
For the body of Christ.

1 Thessalonians 5:5

The Skater ~

Every day he skates,
Down at the skate park.
From dawn to dusk,
He leaves his mark;
Both on the pavement,
And on their hearts.
A teenage legend,
Aspiring to be;
A mentor and friend,
To all he meets.
Sharing the Gospel,
Of repentance and faith.
Christ's young apprentice,
At the skate park today.
He's found practicing tricks,
Or sitting on his board;
Teaching and praying,
Giving praise to the Lord.

1 Timothy 4:12

The Virtuous Woman Collection

LORD, may she wear her purity like a fine garment,
And let her worth be as many rubies!

Proverbs 31:10 & 30

A Glimpse of Sincerity ~

I asked my love if there was another,

And then looked deep into her eyes,

Awaiting an honest reply.

She answered:

...

"My heart knows no lover foreign or near,

Other than you, my heart is sincere."

A glimpse of sincerity I saw in her eyes.

The lover of my youth, my heart's greatest prize.

I thought to myself, an honest woman I have found,

Who is both loyal and true;

No wandering eyes, no clever smile,

Only a dream which continues to come true.

Proverbs 31:11-12

A Lady of Virtue ~

Beneath the flowering trees,
White buds nestled on blue-green leaves,
Dwelling among moss covered stones,
Is a sculpture of a woman who sits all alone.

"A Lady of Virtue,"
her inscription reads;
"A woman of morals,
Who knew no greed.
She loved her children,
and to her husband was true.
She walked with her Lord,
A lady of virtue."

Near a reflection pool her image rests,
In this warm, midsummer breeze.
A fountain reflecting ever so clear,
White buds nestled on blue-green leaves.

Proverbs 31:28

Purified ~

Her sins are forgiven,
In her spiritual baptism;
As she is clothed in purity,
In the garment of Christ.
She is born-again,
Washed and sanctified;
Practicing abstinence,
In the Father's eyes;
Wearing a ring of promise,
Of modest size.

It's a display of righteousness,
Until she marries God's best;
She carries no burdens,
From the life that she left;
Now that she's baptized,
Into Christ's life and death.

Revelation 19:8

What Makes a Woman ~

A girl's beauty is only as deep as her skin;
A woman's beauty radiates from within.
A pretty face makes a lovely girl,
But a heart that loves makes a woman your world.

A girl will play games with your heart.
They don't consider the fire they start,
Or the damage it will do,
To the heart that is true.

A woman understands how to love a man.
She does so with tender hands.
A woman has put away childish games.
Pleasing their man is their ultimate aim.

A girl will argue, complain, and shout,
Then leave you out of the blue.
A woman will talk things out,
And will not easily give up on you.

Proverbs 12:4

The Heart of Romance Collection

LORD, guide us in all our relationships,
And teach us the simplicity of true romance!

Proverbs 5:18-19

Autumn Lovers ~

Strawberry wine,
By the creek we shared,
A glass or two,
On a crisp, fall afternoon.
Laying there on a blanket,
Our fingers entwined.
I drew near to her lips,
As she drew closer to mine.
A strawberry kiss,
And we were lost in a dream;
Two hearts in love,
Two souls embracing.
The fire of passion,
Was the color of every tree;
Above and around us,
Radiant, crimson leaves.

Song of Solomon 3:4

Into the Night ~

A balm of fresh rosemary upon her smooth skin,
Refreshes his senses as he lifts up her chin.
Her sweet cherry lips, press up against his;
While their fingers interlock, down by their hips.
In the midst of the moment, they're lost in time.
Their hearts are beating in unison and rhyme.
The moonlight paints her face,
Through the narrow windowpane,
And illuminates some of the room just the same.
She lowers her head down upon his chest,
And listens carefully to hear every breath.
He wraps his arms around her,
And she closes her eyes.
He whispers "I love you,"
And she lets out a sigh.
Their two engraved champagne glasses,
Sit on the table beside,
Near where their shadows dance into the night.

Song of Solomon 2:3-4

The Proposal ~

Two lovers enjoy the sunrise at low tide,
When they witness an exotic surprise;
Wild horses running along the coastline,
Making for a treasurable moment in time.
Both mares and stallions sprinting free,
Like heavenly thoroughbreds,
Straight from a dream.
The young woman watches,
As if in a trance,
Amazed by the stampede,
And the horses' galloping dance.
As they kick up sand,
Along the turquoise sea,
The young man seizes his opportunity.
With gentle hands, he slowly turns her around,
And falls to his knees,
Upon the sand covered ground;
Telling her that he loves her,
And how she is his dream.
He asks her to marry him,
As he pulls out the ring.

Song of Solomon 1:9

The Tailor of My Dreams ~

I hear her call out to me,
As I walk the meadow of ashwood trees.
Like a residual echo across the mountainside,
Her soul beckons for mine, and I am at her side.
Her whisper rides the meandering wind,
Awakening my senses within;
Giving me courage to face another night,
With unwavering confidence and spiritual sight.
Indeed, she is the tailor of my dreams,
Weaving, shaping, and mending reality.
A soul so innocent and young at heart,
Her spirit flows to where ancient rivers part,
And upon this man, she has left her mark.

Song of Solomon 2:1

The Sea of Grace Collection

Let the waves come, and the torrents of rain;
For my strength is in you LORD, my sea of grace!

Psalm 107:23-24

Anchor of my Soul ~

As I sail across these deep waters,
I will lift my eyes up toward you;
For my hope is placed in no other,
And your hand will guide me through.
When the sea becomes unpassable,
And great waves threaten to devour;
I will call to the anchor of my soul,
"Lord give me strength in this hour!
Keep this vessel afloat on the sea,
As darkened clouds come rolling in;
Anchor me firmly upon my knees,
And deliver thy servant from every sin.
Do not let fear overtake this soul,
Increase my faith throughout the storm;
And I will surrender with righteous hope,
As your love and mercy guides me home."

Hebrews 6:19-20

Beside the Evening Sea ~

She walks the shoreline late at night,
And dreams her dreams beneath the moonlight.
Waiting patiently for her prince to arrive,
A sail to appear above the rolling tide.
Her gown is white against the black night,
Her feet are bare, and love is her only care;
As she walks the shoreline sipping a glass of red wine,
Her long hair blowing in the evening wind,
As she waits earnestly just for him.
Soon he will be with her and embrace her passionately,
Beneath the starry sky, beside the evening sea.

Song of Solomon 1:2

Island of White ~

She's an island of white,
Shining ever so bright,
A beacon of light,
Through the darkest of nights.
And, I am the castaway,
Upon her white sands;
A welcomed guest,
To this once foreign land.

Standing faithful and true,
Amidst a sea of deep blue;
She's an island of white,
In brilliance of light.
And, this island of white,
She continues to shine;
Through the darkest of nights,
A great treasure to find.

Proverbs 30:18-19

Living in a Daydream ~

Another day busy as a bee;
Another day where I don't care to be.
Another moment lost in daydream;
Another day living in a memory.

...I'm barefoot in the sand,
Lying beside my best friend.
It's a smoldering summer day.
I feel the stress melt away.
Sunlight bathes my skin,
As the water greets my feet.
It's another day in paradise,
With the one I love next to me.
Voices of laughter on the wind,
Children playing in the sand;
The waves and seagulls calm me,
As I envision this day by the sea...

Another day resting on the beach;
Another day isn't out of my reach.
Another moment of fun in the sun;
Another day of work is done!

Proverbs 13:12

Sandpiper ~

There is a mostly forgotten myth,
Which survived barely to this day;
About a young master and his bird,
Made of water, sand, and clay.
"Sandpiper, oh sandpiper,
Won't you come alive and play?"
The young master called out,
In the midst of a calming seascape.
Other children laughed with disbelief,
At the sight of the boy and his bird;
But the young master ignored them,
As he again repeated those words:
"Sandpiper, oh sandpiper,
Won't you come alive and play?"
The young master proclaimed,
As he ascended higher in faith.
In a moment everything changed,
By the vibration of what was said;
In that instant the bird came alive,
Scurrying along the water's edge.

~ This poem is based on a myth of young Jesus
in the Lost Books of the Bible and Islamic text.

Sea of Grace ~

He is the anchor of every vessel,
Battered and worn by the waves.
He is the glow of every lighthouse,
Shining brightly, showing the way.
He is the glory of the sunrise,
Heralding in each new day;
And the wind across the waters,
Guiding sails along the way.
He is the joy of every dolphin,
Jumping high and giving praise.
He is the moon pull on the tide,
Telling the waters where to lay.
He is the fullness of the sea,
And we are mere drops you see;
Like wandering vessels,
Weathering storms faithfully.
His wrath is like a hurricane,
His mercy like the calm of its eye;
Filled with the brightness of the sun,
Against the clear blue sky.
He is the hope of every sailor,
Above life's dark and murky waters.
He is the answer to their prayers,
Helping them not to falter.
He is the ocean of Spirit,
And His character, we can't come near it;
Unless we receive Him with faith,
And embrace His sea of grace.

Isaiah 43:16

Seashell Memories ~

As she sits alone on her front porch swing,
In view of the beach and rolling sea;
She reflects on seashell memories.

Recalling the times with her sister again,
Two little girls sifting through the white sand;
Telling seashell secrets, as the closest of friends.
Many seashells they found and admired as gold,
Holding them to their lips, after every secret told.
They talked about the future, and what it might hold;
Dreaming of marriage, and the dress they would wear.
They dreamt their dreams with laughter and care,
Not knowing that life would be so unfair.

Now seashell memories get her through each day,
While she sits and holds each shell, she quietly prays;
And God grants her peace with each passing wave.

Psalm 116:15

She Leaves Me Wanting ~

She leaves me wanting,
Always desiring more.
My love is the ocean,
And hers is the shore.
We embrace every night,
Beneath golden moonlight,
At high tide we're seen,
Manifesting this dream.
Every morning I long,
To meet with her again.
But the lengths of the days,
Are growing longer my friend.
She leaves me wanting,
Wanting for more.
My love is the ocean,
And hers is the shore.

Song of Solomon 8:3

The Great Escape ~

Stranded in the midst of the turquoise sea,
Shipwrecked on the Isle of the Palm Tree;
He scurried down from a canopy of leaves,
From his camouflaged shelter in the trees.

The day had finally arrived for this castaway.
The island had been his home now for many days;
But conditions were right to make his escape,
And down on the beach his chariot did wait.

He reached the makeshift raft and climbed in.
The seaward man glanced back at the island,
Watching the palm trees sway like young maidens,
Waving good-bye to their summer-time companions.

Song of Solomon 7:6-7

The Floral Collection

LORD, manifest around me your Garden of Eden,
And let me partake of the Tree of Life, which is Christ!

Luke 12:27-28

A Garden Sanctuary ~

Through the gates of the garden,
They walk day by day;
Among the pleasant floral,
Of their most sacred place.

It's a sweet, scented sanctuary,
Filled with beauty and life.
A refuge from daily trials,
For the man and his wife.

It's a paradise for their children,
To hide, dance, and play;
And a peaceful place for prayer,
In God's bountiful showcase.

Job 8:16

The Garden Staircase ~

Up the garden staircase,
They walk every afternoon;
Observing the landscape,
In colorful, splendid bloom.

Looking out across the garden,
The elderly couple gaze;
Holding one another close,
As they explore this floral maze.

Hidden amidst a canopy of flowers,
The seasoned lovers reminisce;
Of the time when they first met,
Reenacting love's first kiss.

Song of Solomon 4:16

The Primrose Path ~

On the first day of spring,
Along the primrose path;
He approached a wishing well,
And there, met a young lass.
She was tossing in silver coins,
Wishing for a love that lasts;
When he lost his footing,
Stumbling off the primrose path.
The maiden giggled and smiled,
And let out a short, little laugh;
For he fell into the garden pond,
Beside the primrose path.
"Whom is this fine young lad,
Swimming among the lily pads?"
She sarcastically called to him,
With superficial voice and grin.
But when extending an arm,
To help him out, she too fell in;
And the two began to splash,
Beside that primrose path.

Song of Solomon 6:3

The Beautiful Soul Collection

LORD, let those souls which belong to you,
Find peace in their hearts through and through!

Galatians 5:22-23

A Therapeutic Bath ~

Miniature streams of water flow over her body,
Until she's immersed in a mixture of suds and water.
Her fair complected face reflects the flickering glow
of soft candlelight. She reaches for a handful of bubbles
and softly blows, sending a few floating in the air.
She giggles, leans back, and closes her eyes.
The steady flow of the lukewarm water,
Feels therapeutic over her smooth, delicate skin.
The sound of gentle running water combined,
With the soothing background music;
Only adds to the ambience,
Of this therapeutic bath.

Song of Solomon 4:7

Awaken ~

The world is not at all as it seems.
It's but a reflection of God's dream.
With all things held together,
By Christ's divine consciousness;
A symphony of resonating Spirit,
Arousing those who can hear it.
True faith is so much more,
Than a belief in the unseen;
It's a higher state of reality.
His Spirit is calling out,
Awakening us into the Kingdom of Christ;
Where walls can be passed through,
Great mountains can move,
And the dead can come to life.

Ephesians 5:14

Baptism ~

The sacrament of baptism,
Was established to be;
An outward display,
Of inner purity.

The immersion in water,
Is symbolic indeed;
To the follower of Christ,
A sinner washed clean.

It represents to a disciple,
The death we have in Christ;
And being raised up,
In the newness of life.

Acts 2:38

Cherry Blossom ~

Through the early April rains,
When you first come to bloom;
With bittersweet fragrance,
One early, spring afternoon;
I lift my eyes to behold you,
My tender cherry blossom.
The beauty you display,
Will make for a jealous autumn.
If only you could stay,
All through those summer days;
And taste the crisp of fall,
I wouldn't have to wait too long;
To hold you in these arms,
After winter's snowy charm;
Oh, my tender cherry blossom.

Song of Solomon 2:2

Heavenly Nectar ~

A hummingbird gracefully hovers,
Above petals of a flowering soul;
Tasting of such heavenly nectar,
The sweetest it has ever known.
An awakening of the lotus,
A gift from the Father up above;
A fountain of life-giving Spirit,
Filling this vessel with love.
Salvation and enlightenment,
Manifests as a sacred flower;
Humility uprooting all pride,
With roots planted firmly inside.
A guardian of light remains,
Hovering over a soul born of love;
Who once had pleasure's stain,
Now the sweetest nectar from above.

Song of Solomon 4:11

Ignite ~

True repentance leads to salvation,
For the lost and wayward soul.
The Spirit of God spirals down,
From heaven to earth below.
It descends like a glorious dove,
Once a sinner chooses grace.
The Spirit ignites the soul with love,
And sets the heart ablaze;
Raising us up from dirt and mire,
Above carnal and earthly desire.
It calls us to walk upon the waters,
Upon the deep where darkness covers;
As we accept Christ's sacrifice,
And are born again into eternal life.

Acts 2:3-4

Manifest ~

Through Christ, all things are possible,
And in him all things exist.
He was the vibration spoken at creation,
And God's Word that came in the flesh.
It is through God's Holy Spirit,
And His laws of quantum physics;
Where the faithful can manifest,
Through faith transcendence.
When we increase our frequency,
Mountains can move out of their place;
As the Spirit takes us beyond,
And into that realm of grace;
Where words and thoughts can activate,
And transform the world by faith.

Acts 4:16

Songbird ~

The songbird is beautiful indeed.
When she sings, such blessing it brings,
Like a beautiful angel fluttering heavenly wings,
Surpassing the glory of princes and kings,
To bring a smile to the loneliest child.
How great the voice, how great the worth,
Transforming hearts, bringing peace on earth.
There is no greater thing heard,
Than the voice of a lone songbird.
And, so pleasing it would be,
If she shared her song with me.
Oh, songbird this is where you belong,
Let your voice go forth like an everlasting song.

Song of Solomon 2:12

The Beauty Awakens ~

Has the Beauty awakened from her sleep,
Embracing reality of the awakened state;
Passing through that dream filled gate,
Of equal share of darkness and light,
To come back to animate life?

Indeed it is so, the arousal of her soul.
She opens her eyes, and begins to arise,
Like the mid-summer sun above its horizon.
The beauty awakens to her new reality,
And her soul flies free, ever so free.

Psalm 57:8

The Gospel of Love Collection

LORD, open my mouth like that of a trumpet,
Let your wisdom be heard among the people!

John 3:14-21

Jars of Clay ~

Do you know the LORD,
Who formed these jars of clay?
He didn't just form them,
For mere physical display.
He sees the potential,
Of such empty vessels;
A place for His Spirit to dwell,
Becoming sacred temples.
Overtime these jars get--
Worn, broken, or cracked;
But the one who shaped us,
Can refurbish us back.
The Potter waits patiently,
For when we seek to be filled;
With His life - giving water,
Overflowing and spilled.

2 Corinthians 4:7-12

The Father's Dream ~

Share... share... share... share...
And partake in the Father's dream!
For whenever you give and let go,
An abundance is returned, it seems.

If only we made it our daily practice,
To plant love and generosity;
We may be pleasantly surprised,
By how much love is reaped.

If a family of three share their food,
They may well feed four more;
By eliminating waste and gluttony,
And reaping from Heaven's store.

If those seven then share this truth,
As the Kingdom of Christ radiates;
A multitude of hearts will be moved,
By such loving, compassionate display!

2 Corinthians 9:10

The Gospel ~

Jesus Christ is the narrow road;
The way, the truth, and the life.
No one can come to the Father,
But through the Lamb's sacrifice.
He was the Word of Creation,
Which presides over all things;
Above earthly and heavenly,
Kingdoms, thrones, and beings.
A prince herald by angels,
And testified of in ancient text.
Having been born of a virgin,
Jesus Christ came in the flesh.
He is the light of the world,
The means of our salvation;
Enlightening darkened souls,
And pruning every nation.

John 14:6

The Kingdom of Love ~

The Kingdom of Love,
Can be found within,
Among, and all around those;
Who repent of all sin.
It begins as a spring,
Cleansing us new;
A fountain from the Father,
Flowing through and through.
It waters a sunflower seed,
At the seat of our soul;
Giving us the light of Christ,
To flourish and grow.
As we track with the Spirit,
Journaling every word;
Of wisdom and faith,
To share with the world.
Sowing and reaping,
In the Kingdom of Love;
Living in the son-ship,
Of God's oneness and love.

Mark 10:15

The Shepherd and the Lamb ~

In a lush meadow they stood,
The mother and her two lambs;
At the edge of the dense wood,
How they jumped; how they ran.
Only one had been approved,
Fed and bathed by its mother.
The other kicked and ignored,
As both lambs grew asunder.
The shepherd noticed the behavior,
And the little, poised lamb in need.
He carried the estranged one home,
To bathe, rest, and bottle feed.
It grew up strong and vibrant,
The healthiest one of all three.
This lamb had been adopted,
Into the shepherd's own family.

John 10:14

The Spirit of Love ~

The Spirit of Love,
Comes in the form of a dove.
It makes its descent from heaven,
Possessing the temple of man.

Merging Spirit with spirit,
And lifting consciousness up;
To heightened awareness in Christ,
Overfilling the mortal's cup.

A repentant vessel of earth,
Ascends to find eternal worth;
Now enlightened from above,
Through the Spirit of Love.

2 Timothy 1:7

True Doctrine ~

There is only one God,
The Father of all;
Revealed to us by Jesus,
And acknowledged by Paul.

- John 17:3 & 1 Corinthians 8:6

There is only one mediator,
Between God and sinful man;
The man, Jesus Christ,
In between he always stands.

- 1Timothy 2:5

There is only one Spirit,
Shared by Father and Son;
And everyone who believes,
In what Christ has done.

- Ephesians 4:4 & Romans 8:9

There is only one body,
The body of Christ.
We dwell in the Father,
Through his sacrifice.

1 John 4:13-16

The Storms of Change Collection

Oh LORD, carry me through this storm,
Keep the wind and the waves from overtaking me!

Matthew 7:24-27

Coming Change ~

I can hear the distant thunder.
I see pillars of fire in the sky.
I can feel the wind blowing,
And I know the storm is nigh.
I see clouds gathering on the horizon,
As they deliver a quenching rain.
I behold the rivers rising,
And I know there's coming change.

Jeremiah 30:23

Faith Walks on Water ~

Faith walks on water,
Across the raging sea;
When I hear the Lord,
Calling out to me.

He's calling out my name,
Through the wind and rain;
Telling me to come,
Into his open arms.

Faith walks on water,
And fear has no place;
For he has raised me up,
Into the realm of grace.

Even through the storm,
As great darkness covers;
I see him standing there,
Calling me across the waters.

Matthew 14:22-33

Under Heaven's Dome ~

Under heaven's dome the earth will shake,
Thunder, lightning, and great earthquakes.
The moon will turn red as blood,
And men will hide in fear and run.
The sky will split and Christ will return,
From heaven above descending to earth.
The time is near, the time is nigh,
Keep watch therefore and open your eyes.
The faithful will shine like the sun in the sky,
And God will wipe every tear from their eyes.

Luke 21:28

When He Comes ~

When clouds roll back, and Christ appears,
Amidst the thundering, amidst the tears;
We'll hear a shout, a trumpet sound,
Ringing high above the ground.
We'll lift our eyes unto the skies;
We'll all be changed in a moment's time.

1 Corinthians 15:50-55

The Battle Cry Collection

LORD, I am surrounded by vast armies,
Deliver me from their fiery swords and flaming arrows!

Psalm 20:5

The Battlefield ~

Canons echo through the mountains,
As wind and fire dance.
Another stronghold crumbles and falls;
While a golden flag ascends.
Moving forward, we're gaining ground,
Marching through the range.
Reddish banners wave around,
Above the tainted plain.
Arrows of light cut through the air,
Taking the enemy by surprise;
Penetrating our darkened hearts,
Blemished by sin and lies.
A heavenly cavalry leads the way,
As our spirits march alongside,
Stripping away every temptation,
Of jealousy, lust, and pride.

Galatians 5:16–18

The Children of Light ~

Have you heard about the children of light?
Do you know their unearthly origins;
Those warriors of the Kingdom of Heaven?
They are the personage of Christ himself,
Sown by God's own right hand.
They embody the Father and Son,
And will judge both angels and men.
They are mentioned often in the Bible,
As those who are born of God.
Greater are they than the angels,
Each will rule with an iron rod.
They will be given authority over the nations,
And will shatter them as clay pottery.
Each will be given the morning star,
For this is their truest destiny.

Revelation 2:26-29

Warrior of Yah ~

Warrior of Yah, your victory is nigh,

The enemy is falling, upon the battlefields of life.

For the God of all creation, has always been at your side;

Defending and protecting you, with angels far and wide.

Strongholds of the enemy which were once so fortified,

Are now collapsed and left abandoned;

Amidst the rubble, strong towers lie.

The enemy is in retreat, attempting to escape;

Their final destination, their fiery end and fate.

Warrior of Yah, your victory is at hand,

The enemy that continues against you,

Shall perish in this land.

Ephesians 6:10-18

We Come to You ~

Through the blood and through the pain;
We come to you, we still remain.
You are our strength; you are our shield.
You bring us through the mine filled fields.
You break down strongholds in our path,
You give us victory upon the cliff.
Through the flood and through the flame;
We come to you, we still remain.

Isaiah 43:2

The Darkened Night Collection

In the darkest night, I shall not fear,
For you light the way and I will trust in you, LORD!

John 12:46

Haunted by the Ghosts Within ~

The ghosts from her past,
Walk the halls of her memories.
Passageways lined with distorted mirrors,
Warped visions of yesterday.
They remain a constant reminder,
Which frightens her to this day.
The skeletons in her closets,
Dwell in darkened depths of consciousness;
And she can't seem to escape,
The inner guilt, and self-hate.
Her thoughts lurk in ghastly corridors,
Hearing voices from ages ago;
A distant and residual echo,
Continues to torment her soul.
She's trapped in a labyrinth,
Inner chambers lined with doors.
Each one opens to a half empty room,
With furniture draped of linen and dust.
They represent the past she's covering up.
If she would only surrender, forgive herself,
And cry out to the Lord for help;
Perhaps one who loves would hear her,
And help her find her way out;
Out of this castle of illusion,
Haunted by her past,
That her fears have distorted,
Where darkened shadows are now cast.

Psalm 139:11-12

The Black Rose ~

Her bowsprit pierces true,
Penetrating the shadowy mist;
As she navigates her way through,
A shallow graveyard of half sunken ships.

Her tattooed crew was almost lynched,
But through trickery escaped the gallows.
The mastermind was Captain Bentz,
Who freed his seafaring fellows.

Their destination the Isle of Skulls,
Where their guarded fortress lies.
The treasure they carry aboard her hull,
Silver and gold from ancient times.

It's now kept safe by soulless renegades,
And British cannons at her side.
The Black Rose once Britain's Rose,
Has found her destiny through demise.

Isaiah 33:23

The Black Widow ~

The black widow is what they called her,
A wandering and darkened heart;
Laying a web of fine lies and afterwards...
..bitter words and broken hearts.
Her poison was her beauty,
And, that's how she entraps.
A master of seduction,
She lures in unexpecting hearts.
A lethal dose injection,
And the soul of man departs.
I'm counted among the few,
That ever has escaped;
The beauty of the black widow,
And her venomous trap of fate.

Proverbs 5:3-6

The Nightingale's Lullaby ~

If you listen closely from the depths of the night,
When deep, darkness covers and there's but little light;
You may perchance hear the nightingale's lullaby.
Once his call goes forth through the air of the night,
As the atmosphere appears like the thinnest of veils;
Upon the wind is heard, the song of the nightingale.
As the crescent, pale moon shines its faintest of light,
And low clouds beneath consume all things in sight;
The nightingale's lullaby may alone ease your mind.

Proverbs 27:8

***A Night in Englewood Cemetery ~

The entrance to Englewood Cemetery seemed far from inviting. It was guarded by two lightly snow covered and cracked, marble images, of what appeared to be fallen angels. The cold rusted gates and frozen weeping willow trees nearby, only added to the discomfort of the boys. The two brothers swallowed their pride, determined to make it through a single winter's night, in Englewood Cemetery.

Just before midnight, they made their way through the gates, taking with them only a flashlight and some blankets for warmth. This would ensure they followed the dare, which they now seemed to forlorn. They have been warned about the gravedigger's ghost, who was rumored to arrive shortly after the stroke of midnight. So they agreed to keep watch together for that first hour.

Midnight came and went, with no signs of a ghost; still the boys huddled together, waiting in nervous anticipation. After all, there were numerous other distractive creature sounds in the darkness, other than that of imaginary ghosts. As the night went on, the boys were startled by the piercing caw of a black crow. They spotted the bird perched upon the shoulder of an ice covered statue of a child. This statue seemed creeper than the rest, perhaps due to the cracked face and missing right arm. The boys noticed even more fearfully, what looked like an unearthed grave beneath this frozen tribute.

Nervously, they decided to check out the freshly opened grave, moving ever closer to the edge. As they gazed steadily into the black abyss, they heard a frightening moan behind them, and both boys lost their footing and fell into the shallow grave. Looking up they saw what appeared to be a large silhouette of a man, with a shovel in his right hand. The boys screamed as if someone in the vicinity could hear their call for help, but they were a couple miles out from town, and there weren't any houses nearby.

The boys held each other as they yelled, and the man gave out another billowing moan and lifted up his shovel…

..But then extended it outward and told the boys to climb out. Once out of the grave, the younger of the two brothers exclaimed "Well you're no ghost!" The man who was now seen to be middle aged, with a well-worn beard and rugged overcoat, just laughed. "Of course I'm no ghost. We have been having a problem with vandals, and I have been keeping watch here at night, while digging graves for the cemetery. Why don't you boys go run along home now and get warmed up, I'm sure your parents are concerned about you." The boys sighed with great relief, thanked the man, and headed home.

Proverbs 12:25

The Love is Forever Collection

LORD, let my love for her be strong like a cedar,
And let my heart flow as a spring flows from the earth!

Song of Solomon 8:6-7

If Only I Could Fly ~

If only I could fly,
I'd embrace you in these arms of mine;
And take you up and away,
Far above both land and wave.
We would soar, ever so high,
Like the stars in Heaven's sky;
And dance amidst their light,
Into the star filled night.
I would show you a greater love,
Beyond the things that dreams are made of;
And I'd carry you further away,
To a secret island hideaway.
I'd show you the beauty of each tomorrow,
As we rise above life's sorrow;
To that place of amazing grace,
Where human hearts are freed,
And all consciousness is raised.

Esther 2:16-17

The Language of Love ~

Romance is the language of love.
It sends the heart soaring,
Like the young mourning dove.
A rose in a box,
Some sweet candlelight;
Soft love songs playing,
A gentle kiss, goodnight.
A warm bubble bath,
Will make her heart light;
And holding her close,
All through the night.
A note "I love you,"
Or a simple whisper will do.
It's the little things,
Which go a long way;
And give her butterflies,
Throughout her day.
A horseback ride in the mountains,
Along a winding trail,
Holding her hand,
Or lifting her wedding veil;
A kiss in a lighthouse,
Overlooking the sea,
A dance in the rain,
Beneath an old, oak tree.
Lying beside her,
On a cloudless, starry night;
Is where the language of love,
Will always feel right.

Song of Solomon 2:3-4

Violets Are Forever ~

A meadow flower of bluish hue,
Purple violets, spring up true.
For my love, I pick a few;
Beyond April's rain and dew.
As we walk that field together,
In the loveliest, sunny weather;
I tell her, as violets I gather,
Love and violets are forever.
Amused, she decorates her hair,
Amidst clouds of violets there;
An angel with her feet left bare,
Walks beside me, ever so fair.

Song of Solomon 2:10-13

Waterfront Romance ~

Waterfront romance,
Is a getaway for two;
To this charming, southern city,
Where there's always something to do.
You may stroll along the riverwalk,
Beside the great Cape Fear;
Where you can talk all through the night,
With the one that you hold dear.
You may enjoy a sunset dinner cruise,
With the finest glass of wine;
Or a restaurant on the water's edge,
Might be your choice to dine.
You may ride a horse drawn carriage,
Along historical, stoned roads;
And stroll through quaint galleries,
Where sweetheart gifts are sold.
Or leave footprints in the sand,
As you walk beneath a pier;
Enjoying carefree romance,
Until the morning sun appears.

Song of Solomon 7:10

The Family Collection

Thank you for those who are nearest to me.
Let your Spirit LORD, protect and deliver all my family!

Psalm 128:3

I Am My Brother's Keeper ~

I am my brother's keeper.
I will always lend him a hand.
I will defend him with honor,
And value his reputation.
I will stand up beside him,
Never will he stand alone.
I am my brother's keeper.
I'll always welcome him home.
I will sacrifice much for him,
And never bring him down.
I am my brother's keeper,
And I'll always be around.
I am my brother's keeper.
When in need, I will be there.
I will bring him encouragement,
With kindness, love, and care.

1 John 4:20

In the Hands of Love ~

Ever since I entered this world,
I've been in the hands of love;
Whether that love was displayed,
On the shoulders of my father,
Or in the arms of my mother;
That love was ever present,
Though difficult at times;
When discipline was necessary,
Firm guidance I would find.
But mercy and love,
Continued to show through;
Leading me down,
The road of grace and truth;
All while in the hands of love.

Proverbs 22:6

Letters from Home ~

Camped out on the frontlines,
Somewhere in the unknown;
He sits in a makeshift shelter,
Reading letters from home.

These letters are a treasure,
Helping him to go on;
In this war torn place,
Far from parents, wife, and son.

Every day he would sit,
And read them once again;
These letters from home,
Brought such Inspiration.

They gave him comfort,
Until the very end;
When God called him away,
And his Bible went to a friend.

His friend found and read,
Those letters from home;
He inherited a loving family,
And is no longer alone.

John 15:13

Seashell Memories ~

As she sits alone on her front porch swing,

In view of the beach and rolling sea;

She reflects on seashell memories.

Recalling the times with her sister again,

Two little girls sifting through the white sand;

Telling seashell secrets, as the closest of friends.

Many seashells they found and admired as gold,

Holding them to their lips, after every secret told.

They talked about the future, and what it might hold.

Dreaming of marriage, and the dress they would wear.

They dreamt their dreams with laughter and care,

Not knowing that life would be so unfair.

Now seashell memories get her through each day,

While she sits and holds each shell, she quietly prays;

And God grants her peace with each passing wave.

Romans 14:8

She Dances With Butterflies ~

She dances with butterflies,
At the tender age of twelve;
Such an innocent life,
Filled with wonder and love.

She dances with butterflies,
And the world stands still;
She reaches towards the sky,
In a field of daffodils.

After years have gone by,
She gets lost in his eyes;
Placing her hands on his side,
She dances with butterflies.

She dances with butterflies,
To their wedding song;
Soon memories are made,
With children of their own.

She dances with butterflies,
At a tender old age.
Her children are grown,
And her memory fades.

She dances with butterflies,
And the world stands still;
She reaches towards the sky,
In a field of daffodils.

2 Corinthians 5:17

The Freedom from Judgment Collection

Give me the understanding not to judge others, LORD,
And protect me from the judgments of my enemies!

Matthew 7:1-3

Freedom of Religion ~

Freedom of religion is granted to everyone.

It's in our constitution, Amendment number one.

It's the reason so many fought, and many gave their lives;

It shouldn't be taken for granted, belittled, or denied.

It allows for beliefs of all types, with few restrictions on these.

It's every citizen's civil right, to exercise all that they believe.

Joshua 24:15

If Everyone had a Rainbow ~

If everyone had a rainbow,
The world would be a brighter place;
If we all sowed God's Spirit,
And reaped both mercy and grace.

If no one judged another,
And we all just loved each other;
There'd be no more hate or fear,
For we would seldom shed a tear;
If everyone had a rainbow,
And God's Son was reigning here.

Genesis 9:13

Love Them Just Because ~

Some ignore them because they curse, and label them
perverse. They talk about their tattoos, hoodies, or the
rainbows on their shirts; never caring to get to know
them, and love them just because; they were made in
the Creator's image, instead they only judge.

If Jesus came back today, we may be quite surprised,
about what he'd do and say, and who he'd accept and
deny. You see God alone knows the hearts of men,
and only He can save, so try living out the Gospel in
a positive, loving way. Don't talk about the drink in
their hand, or the way in which they dress; let them
know that all have sinned, and God offers mercy and
rest. Quit worrying about what someone says, or what
another person does; for we are commanded to love
every one of them just because!

Genesis 1:26-27

Please Forgive Me ~

Please forgive me, I make mistakes.
I'm only human for heaven's sakes.
When I stumble, don't keep me down.
When I fall, help me off the ground.
Sometimes I'm blind and cannot see,
Please, please forgive me.

Please forgive me when I say,
Words that harm, if I'm having a bad day.
Please respond with a smile and heart,
It's your opportunity to leave your mark.
Love is the key to change you see,
So please, please forgive me.

Please forgive me, sometimes I hurt,
And can't escape, lower realities of pain and hate.
Whenever I sink into the pit of negativity,
Please help me out, and please forgive me.

Psalm 25:11

Where Grace Abounds ~

How vital it is to call sin, sin;
Always speaking the truth with love.
You never know if someone is listening,
Ready to receive grace from above.

Count it joy when persecution comes,
And know you are on the right track;
If you speak truth from God's Word,
And the world responds with attack.

Remember to judge only behavior,
And not the individual themselves.
For if we don't have love for others,
Then we bring sin upon ourselves.

Always use the words of Scripture,
The Spirit will testify of itself.
We must remain certain and sure,
That we share in wisdom's wealth.

Remember, if people don't hear truth,
Sin will forever tie them down;
And they'll never come to that place,
Where love and mercy abounds.

Ephesians 4:15

The Loneliness Collection

LORD, be my ever present companion,
Guiding me along your paths of righteousness!

Isaiah 41:10

He Gave You Yesterday ~

He gave you yesterday, and yesterday was true,
But is yesterday enough to pull you through?
Will it warm you through those lonely nights,
Now that he's not there to hold you tight?
Will it keep you hoping and longing for more,
Of what yesterday once held in store?
Yesterday came and went,
Its time in history has now been spent,
But what if every day could be like yesterday,
Filled with excitement, love and happiness?
What if every day was a new adventure,
Photographic and spontaneous?
Imagine each brand new day,
With growing success along the way,
And every night feeling more alive,
Because love is no longer a rollercoaster ride.
A new reality awaits you today,
If only you say goodbye to yesterday.

Philippians 3:13

The Celestial Dance ~

A throng of evening stars,
Sing Thy praises at night;
Frolicking angelic princes
Of white marbled light,
Unhindered by a veil
Of air and thin cloud.
Their flames pirouette thro'
Thy black, darkened shroud.
LORD, let Thy radiant sons
Of purest, luminous light;
Keep the loneliest of souls,
Company this night.
May he marvel aloud,
Of such celestial dance,
And be found down below
In elate, jovial prance.

Isaiah 40:26

The Illusion of Loneliness ~

You may feel lonely, but you're never alone;
You may feel lost, but you're always at home.
Just open your eyes, and see past the lies.
There are many angels beside you,
Waiting patiently to guide you;
Messengers of God, wanting you to see,
How the Gospel of Christ can set a soul free.

Reality can change and turn on a dime,
If you awaken from the perception of time.
The circumstances around you are not as they seem,
A positive outlook can alter the dream.
Just remain calm and confident, and you will soon see;
How the world around you, changes to be…
..The life of your dreams.

So draw near to the LORD,
And He will draw close to you.
Wait patiently with faith, for the trials to be through.
Then the mountains will move, and the Earth fade away,
As you step into the Kingdom of God's glorious grace.

Psalm 23:4

The Story of the Crosses ~

Once a man walked alone in the city,
Filled with self-grief, sorrow, and pity.
He didn't realize who he would meet;
A stranger beside the once busy street.

"Do you believe in God, my friend?"
The stranger asked the younger man;
Who gave a heartfelt and honest reply,
"In this city, sir, I've seen no sign."

The stranger knew that the man was lost,
And pointed above the street to a cross.
"Jesus Christ is the light of the world.
He hung on a cross, on Calvary's hill."

"When you're lonely, and physically grieved,
Look to the power lines above the street;
For Jesus is our power line giving us sight,
When we repent and walk in his light."

The words of the stranger seemed so wise.
Unknown to the man, the angel in disguise.
Thanking the Lord for life's gains and losses,
The man headed home counting the crosses.

1 Peter 2:24

Through Shades of Blue ~

Through a veil of deep blue,
There's a way, honest and true.
Beyond a constant rain,
A light beyond the pain.

A destination worthwhile,
Though I travel many miles;
Through a world that is lost,
Filled with heartache and trials.

Still, I continue this journey,
Through shades of blue.
Seeking God's luminous light,
Beyond this ocean of blue.

Ezekiel 27:7

You'll Never Walk Alone ~

A father once told his son: "Son, you'll never walk alone,
Even though you venture out, far away from home.
For deep within your heart you'll find,
Reason for life's song and rhyme.
My love you hold inside you, will help to always guide you;
through good and troublesome days,
As you learn to walk in my ways."

The son replied: "Father, I know you won't ever leave me,
Until I reach my journey's end.
I know you'll go with me, as I teach and heal each man.
Within my heart I'll carry you, over land and over sea;
Until that moment of atonement, upon Calvary's lonely tree.
Through my blood all sins will be atoned,
So that other's will hear the words, You'll never walk alone."

Luke 5:15-16

The Ancient Treasures Collection

From the vast treasuries and libraries of the ancients,
LORD, grant me a wealth of wisdom!

Daniel 7:22

***Amidst Stones of Fire ~

Lumen and the one third of angelic host built up mountains of fire in the midst of paradise. They did so with the help and specifications that Yhovah sent via his archangels. For these mountains were to be witnesses in the land, for as long as earth shall last, holding the secrets of that which was to come; secrets that not even the angels themselves fully understood.

Lumen chose the greatest and most illuminated mountain for his governing throne, which was an obvious representation of the mountain of Yhovah that has its place in the highest heaven. Even the capstone was shaped like the holiest tabernacle which is above. Lumen began his assigned work as a watchman over the Garden of Yhovah, by establishing an angelic governing body, mirroring the one in heaven. The greatest mountain of fire was constructed at the center of all the earth's land mass, and became known as the great mountain of paradise; as well as, the earthly symbol of the heavenly mountain of Yhovah. Lumen assigned the powers to guard his throne, much in the way that he once guarded the throne of the almighty, on the mountain of Yhovah above. Lumen, then ordered his angels to their new duties in the Garden of Yhovah, and stationed certain hierarchy to govern the different land areas across earthly paradise.

Paradise flourished and Lumen went up to the mountain of Yhovah on occasion, to report back all that he had accomplished. Every time Lumen would return, many of the holy angels would take council at the foot of the mountain of Yhovah, in hopes to hear about the Garden of Yhovah and earthly paradise below, which many of them seldom, if ever saw.

- An excerpt from Chad's upcoming Bible based fantasy novel **Through the Gates of Eden**

Ancient Words ~

Ancient words,
Of days gone by;
Knowledge withheld
From former times.

Mysterious revelations,
Hidden within;
Religious declarations,
Parable, proverb, & poem.

Coded verse,
And words of prophecy;
Awakening those,
Who have fallen asleep.

Preparing the world,
For what is to come;
And establishing hope,
In the righteous one.

Amos 3:7

Dreamweaver ~

Precious glowing pearls flicker in the evening sky,
A multi-colored kaleidoscope of all spectrum of light;
Dancing above this awe-inspiring world of dreamscapes.
Gardens fill with mysterious mist, after a purple storm;
Once brought on by rain music of white angelic beings.
Smiling the Dreamweaver introduces His next spectacle,
A floating city constructed of crystalized, transparent gold.
The city proceeded down touching the new earth,
And the mountain of God was opened up to all immortals.

Exodus 20:18 & Rev. 21:2

Jacob's Ladder ~

~ Solomon once gave great wisdom.
There is nothing new under the sun;
Whatever is here has been here before.
Such wisdom should not be ignored.
Ecclesiastes 1:10

~ God's righteous and faithful servant Job,
Once shared an even stranger truth:
Naked from my mother's womb, I came,
And naked I will return there again.
Job 1:21

~ Jacob, God's chosen one of Israel,
Had a vision of angels upon a ladder.
The angels ascended and descended,
On the Son of Man to and from heaven.
John 1:51

~ The greatest man was John the Baptist,
And if the Word of God is proof;
Jesus said for all who can receive it,
John the Baptist is Elijah in truth.
Matthew 11:11-14

~ Christ was the root and offspring of David,
The first Adam was a soul, and the last a Spirit.
Jesus Christ is both the first and the last,
For all those who can truly hear it!
Rev. 22:16

The Elixir of Life ~

The elixir of life,
Is not what you think;
It is truly a spice,
Not liquid or drink.

In ancient times,
It was worth more than gold,
A rare and treasured find,
With benefits untold.
Revered by ruling kings,
And the greatest of wise men;
For the vast healing it brings,
This gift known as cinnamon.

Song of Solomon 4:14

The Fountain of Youth ~

In brilliance of light,

Upon a majestic peak;

Through a haunting mist,

An ancient city sits.

It's from days long passed,

A time traveler's task;

Unraveling the mystery,

Of this illuminated city.

Hidden in its midst does lie,

A secret much older than time.

In a mystical garden oasis,

Veiled by wild moss and vine;

Beyond the gates of Eden,

Welling up beneath the city of gold;

A spiritual life-giving fountain,

With its healing stories untold.

Revelation 22:1

Voices of Hope ~

Voices of hope
I hear in my mind,
Testimonies of the faith,
Echo through time.

Memories of the past,
Now edged in my soul,
Inspiring words,
Worth more than gold.

Wisdom for the trials,
Still yet to come,
Retrievable knowledge,
From elegant tongues.

Timeless counsel,
From ages past.
Spiritual guidance,
That forever will last.

Hosea 12:10

The Heart of Prayer Collection

Help me to make time for you, LORD,
As I go about my day, may I pray without ceasing!

Matthew 21:21-22

A Life of Prayer ~

A life of prayer,
Is precious indeed;
It moves great mountains,
Manifesting God's dream.
A display of righteousness,
In eyes that can see;
Humbling prideful hearts,
And setting souls free.
Bringing praise to the LORD,
From those who received;
The Gospel of Truth,
By an example of peace.
A life of prayer,
Is lived in humility;
As the world is transformed,
From down on our knees.

Ephesians 6:18

In the Spirit of Nehemiah ~

In the Spirit of Nehemiah,
Send this call across the land;
In the presence of the King of Kings,
And in the sight of every man.
Let us mourn for all our sins,
Praying and fasting many days;
And build up this great wall,
With all its mighty gates.
In the Spirit of Nehemiah,
We await the LORD's promise;
To gather us together again,
And make His nation prosperous.

Nehemiah 1:4-11

Into His Presence ~

In the chamber of shadows,
We track with the LORD;
Through depths of consciousness,
We meditate on His Word.

Focusing on His promises,
In this vision filled state;
Entering the Holy of Holies,
Into the presence of His grace.

We come boldly before the throne,
Wearing the garment of Christ;
Petitioning the Father of Spirits,
Through His all-consuming light.

Hebrews 4:16

The Heart of Prayer ~

With a heart of prayer,
I call upon the LORD;
In this place of solitude,
For these sins I mourn.
Beyond the sight of men,
Witnessed by angelic spies;
Beholding my confessions,
As teardrops fill my eyes.
I seek mercy from the LORD,
For this soul of mine;
And repentance for the flesh,
Which delays my growth in Christ.
As I fast and pray in silence,
I feel your Spirit start;
It enters through my crown,
And fills my prayerful heart.

Romans 10:1

The Lake Sanctuary ~

Down at his lake sanctuary,
The young boy arrives;
Shortly before the dawn,
Awaiting a magical sunrise.

He stares down at his reflection,
Upon the gentle wake;
Stirred by passing fishing boats,
On this peaceful lake.

Like a friend he talks with God,
In a prayer spoken out loud.
He seeks guidance for today,
And with faith brings forth a smile.

The sun appears over the waters,
Growing brighter every moment now;
As he experiences God's Kingdom,
Embracing Christ in the here and now.

1 Peter 5:6

The Life Legacy Collection

LORD, may my life be a beacon of light,
Showing the way like a lighthouse on the shoreline!

Proverbs 20:7

A Grandfather's Legacy ~

He could not make a practice,
And he had never seen a game;
So her mother drove her over,
To see their grandpa once again.

She got in her tee-ball uniform,
And placed her pink helmet on;
She showed him both her swings,
First the short and then the long.

"My child here is a special dollar,
Now you have to make a homerun."
His weary eyes told the story,
Of how he wished he could come.

But little did they both know,
This time he would be watching;
As she made her way across home plate,
He smiled at her through Heaven's gates.

Proverbs 17:6

A True Legacy ~

I wish I were a singer, but I cannot sing.

I wish I had some rhythm, to enjoy some type of dancing.

If only I had the ability, to carry a marvelous tune,

And play guitar or piano, as music fills the room.

But I'm a lowly poet, who speaks often of love,

My words you may not know it,

But I seek them from above.

I wish I were a painter, I'd sit and paint all night,

And if only I could illustrate, I could bring my work to life.

I wish I were an athlete, but I wasn't built that way.

I've often thought of acting, but never starred in a play.

I'm just a lowly poet, and that is fine by me.

All I'm holding onto is living out God's dream.

The moral of my story, is do what you do best.

Focus on your legacy, my friend,

And let God handle all the rest.

Ephesians 4:7

Heart to Heart ~

Heart to heart
And soul to soul,
I'm finding strength,
And want the world to know;
That while you trod
Upon the high road,
And I tread upon the low,
Your legacy lives on,
I carry it as I go.
The good times we had,
Far outweigh all the bad.
All those memories left behind,
Remain present in my mind.
Yet, you are still with me,
And how great the journey,
Through many trials,

(Continued...)

Across many miles,
We'll travel together,
Through stormy,
And sunny weather;
Around many bends,
Up and down every hill,
You're my guardian angel,
And I will trust in God still.
Heart to heart,
And soul to soul,
Your legacy will be seen,
Wherever I go.

2 Corinthians 5:8

My Beautiful, Infant Son ~

Words cannot express,
The pain that I feel.
The loss of you, son,
It feels so surreal.
You are the bright star,
In my darkest night.
I receive from afar,
Your love and your light.
And, yet you are near,
Residing in my heart.
Son, in a special way,
We're never apart.
My life has changed,
And it was God's will.
Your legacy will go on,
I will carry it still.
Until the day that I die,
The world will know you.
Son, it is my promise,
One that I will hold true.

(Continued...)

God knows the reason,
He took you away.
Son, as hard as it is,
I know you couldn't stay.
Now you go before me,
To prepare a heavenly space;
As I continue your legacy,
Throughout this earthly place.
All life has its purpose,
And I'm starting to understand.
This is only the beginning,
Of God's master plan.
Sometimes I feel defeated,
But I know the victory is won;
For I'm living out the legacy,
Of my beautiful, infant son.

Matthew 19:14

The Legacy I Live ~

This legacy I live, I live it for you.
With each forward step, it comes more into view;
In every passing moment, it will manifest anew,
An aspect of your dream come true.
With nothing to stop it, hinder, or undue;
Your Kingdom, LORD, is continually on the move.
I must align my talents, gifts, and desires;
Feed the flame of the Holy Spirit's fire.
For the time is now and the need, ever dire;
For the Spirit of Love, to raise me up from the mire.

Psalm 40:2

The Legacy of Spirit ~

Spirit is her name,
Running wild and untamed,
As the wind moves through her mane.
Her beauty few could compare,
And even fewer would ever dare,
To tread those fields of sugarcane,
Where Spirit runs and reigns.
How I long to go with her,
And make her dreams my own.
If only I can be untamed,
And permit my soul to roam.
I could go with Spirit anywhere,
And she'd never feel alone.
We would jump that fence with confidence,
And make every pasture our home.

John 3:8

The World Changers ~

There is a line drawn in the sand,
A spiritual revolution, now at hand.
As forward dreamers, once held down.
Our legacy now must be found.

Let us go beyond the boundaries,
Our enemies have set in place.
Let us strive to fulfill our purpose,
As one body bound by grace.

For we are the chosen ones,
Redeemed from all the earth.
A spiritual network of rising suns,
Called out from a worldly church.

Romans 8:29

The Spirit of Christmas Collection

LORD, let us experience the Spirit of Christ,
All throughout the year, and let our giving be bountiful!

Isaiah 9:6

A Christmas of Love ~

Beyond all the sparkles,
Of soft Christmas lights;
A lowly stranger shivers,
On Christmas Eve night.
Upon the park bench,
All laden with snow;
On a cold winter's night,
He sits all alone.
Many will pass him by,
Not giving it a thought.
Some more than once,
Will laugh or will scoff.
Only a few will ever notice,
That twinkle in his eye;
For only hearts led by love,
Help angels in disguise.
A Christmas of love,
He waits for this night;
As people pass by,
Beneath the street light.

Hebrews 13:2

A Star Is Born ~

A star is born this Christmas Eve,
A little angel, Heaven receives.
On the wings of God's Spirit,
She ascends upon high,
To dwell in the oneness,
Of the eternal Christ.
A soul delivered,
Her spirit now freed.
A gift for the heavens,
Free of suffering and grief.
A star is born this Christmas Eve!

Daniel 12:3

Upon a Bed of Snow ~

Beneath the evening pearl,
The lesser of two lights,
In southern Appalachia,
On a snowy winter's night;
Two lovers embrace,
Holding each other close;
As two souls meet playfully,
Upon a bed of snow.
It's a winter wonderland,
In the Blue Ridge Mountains;
Outside the small log cabin,
With an ice covered fountain.
Giggling and whispering,
Beneath a lamp light's glow;
Two rosy face lovers gleam,
Upon a bed of snow.

Psalm 147:16

The Cloth Remained ~

The cloth remained from where the babe once laid,
Reminding them of the one who saves.
A child of Heaven and a child of Earth,
A newborn king of humble birth.
His cloth was left lying in a manger,
A reminder of the Savior.
For the salvation of men he came,
And in that manger the cloth remained.

The cloth remained from where his body once laid,
Reminding them of the one who saves.
A man of Heaven and a man of Earth,
On a tree he was hung and cursed.
His cloth was left lying in a tomb,
A reminder of his everlasting truth.
For the salvation of men he came,
And in that grave the cloth remained.

The cloth remained left by babe and left by man,
A token of his love, and the revealing of God's plan.

John 20:5-8

The Jingle of the Bells ~

Young lad, what does this sound foretell,
The jingle, the jingle of the bells?
Most assuredly not a time to buy or sell,
Rather time to give thanks and wish well!
Young lad, what does this sound foretell,
The jingle, the jingle of the bells?
Why it's the season of Christ indeed,
A time of merriment for souls set free!
It's the call of charitable compassion,
Praises to sing and sermons to tell;
Young lad, what jubilant noise,
The jingle, the jingle of the bells!

Zechariah 14:20

The Snow Scene ~

Snowflakes repeatedly kiss her blushy cheeks,
While she frolics beneath the ice dressed trees,
Leaving tiny footprints in the snow;
With long hair flowing and face all aglow.

She's a little angel on heaven's clouds,
A pirouetting lass, with a cheerful smile.
She gracefully twirls in a winter wonderland,
With short top boots and mittens on her hands.

Job 37:6

Welcoming the New Year ~

Another year has gone by, and a new one has now come.

It's a time for us to reflect, and a time for us to move on.

This year too will one day pass by, so enjoy the moments,

for time will fly. There will be laughter and tears, memories

will be made for latter years. Successes and failures will be

present too, make the best of them all, and they'll benefit you.

Reach out to give more, plant good seed for heavenly store.

Strive to make your enemies, your friends; at very least,

learn to love them. Time is too short and life is a gift, so use

this New Year to make the most of it!

Ephesians 4:22-24

Proverbs by the Author:

~ LORD, I ask this one thing…
   ..Give me the faith, wisdom, and confidence I need to overcome every temptation.

~ Christ becomes the higher self of every believer. We dwell in him, and he dwells in us. What we do to the least of his people, we do it to ourselves, and we do it to Christ.

~ Pay close attention to the environment around you. Some doors will be opened; others will be closed. Don't waste your time attempting to open doors that the LORD has closed, nor invest your energy in closing doors that the LORD has opened. Your path has been laid out for you, if you choose to walk in it.

~ Once awakened, you will begin to awaken others into the Kingdom of Christ.

~ Miracles happen once faith has been activated. Increase your positive vibration, through Scripture reading and daily meditation.

~ When you desire something, you are telling the world that you are in need of it. Faith is absent from desire, because faith is not a belief that you will acquire something; rather, it is the understanding that you have already acquired it in the LORD.

~ The more you desire something, the harder it is to obtain it. The reason being is that desire carries with it a certain amount of doubt. Be filled with the Spirit of Christ and find contentment and joy in every moment. Then the floodgates of heaven will be opened, and every good thing will flow to you.

~ If the Spirit of the LORD has entered in, then the veil has been torn. You may now enter within your tabernacle, and boldly approach the throne of God.

~ A life built on earthly pleasure is likened to a house of cards. At any given time it can topple down from the slightest false movement.

~ If you earnestly and continually seek truth, it will come to you. It will be like a glorious reunion with a long, lost companion.

~ Whenever the choice presents itself of choosing either wisdom or knowledge; the humble will always choose wisdom, and the prideful will always choose knowledge.

~ Where some people see a brick wall; others see a path surrounded by beautiful flowers. Whatever is seen, felt, and experienced becomes reality for that individual. Therefore, how we perceive the world around us makes all the difference in the world.

~ It was when I aligned my dream with God's dream, that I started seeing my success. Sometimes we hear that we must abandon our dream. This however is rarely true. God gave us our talents, desires, and resources to use. His way is often a parallel road, which won't lead you to a dead end. All you have to do is merge my friend.

~ The mind will typically be somewhat logical, but the heart is easily drawn away by passion and desire. Therefore, when it comes to love, follow your mind; when it comes to your dreams, follow your heart; and in all things do it for the glory of the LORD!

~ What is destined to be can never be changed. Any attempt to change it, will become a stepping stone in the process toward full manifestation.

~ People are like flowers. Once they bloom, the world becomes a more beautiful place.

~ A kingdom with bridges, but no walls, cannot stand. It is not a kingdom at all. A kingdom with walls, but no bridges, cannot expand. It is a kingdom ever small.

~ I will not look upon another person and view them the way they are; but rather, I will see them as if they were living to their fullest potential, if by chance that vision would help manifest positive change in us all.

~ God gives us resources, natural talents, spiritual gifts, inner desires, personal experiences, and time; then He sits back and watches what we do with them all. The wise servant will use these things to live out greater potential in Christ, and the wicked will do nothing.

~ "The first Adam was made a living soul, and the last Adam was made a life-giving Spirit" Paul's words were not referring to two separate men; but rather, of two separate natures. Christ is the first and the last, the root and the offspring of David, and the beginning and ending of God's creation.

~ The flesh is against the Spirit, and the Spirit is against the flesh. Whichever one you feed, is the one that will ultimately succeed.

~ Christ turned water into wine, multiplied fish and bread, walked on the water, moved unseen through a crowd, traveled through physical walls, opened the eyes of the blind, healed the sick, and raised the dead. You believe all of this, but do you believe when he told you that you will do these things, and even greater things than these? I tell you the truth, to receive this requires a faith the size of a grain of sand.

~ Often times the food we take into our bodies, have a direct relation to the behavior that comes after. Eating light can help us ascend spiritually to a higher level of faith in Christ (It is best to avoid meats and processed sugars). Our bodies are temples and God has given us all things, but our flesh can delay our spiritual maturing through eating heavy processed or hormone filled foods. Healing can only take place through ascension in faith, and that can happen almost immediately through a change in diet.

~ The spirit of every man returns to the Father who sent it, their flesh becomes as dust in the earth, and their soul alone hangs in the balance. Yet if a believer dies, in Christ he will yet live.

~ There is no death, no sickness, and no sin in Christ; therefore, rise up from your graves and come up hither!

Author's Baptism Testimony:

*"I'm here to be baptized today. I was baptized as an infant
and I just want to reaffirm my faith, now since I've grown
in the faith, and matured in the faith. To me baptism is an
important step. It represents dying to yourself, and coming
back out of the water alive and renewed. So, I asked Michael
if he would baptize me in this beautiful spot, just flowing with
God's beauty and grace. I just want to reaffirm my faith, be an
example to others, and just show my dedication and my love of
Christ, and be baptized into the baptism of Christ."*

~ Jul 8, 2011

youtube.com/watch?v=o0WWFSpjJ1E

Bonus Poetry Section

Featuring Poetry of Family & Friends

Life is a Roller Coaster ~

Life is a roller coaster.
Life is sometimes as quiet as the ocean surroundings;
Life is sometimes as loud as a herd of elephants.
Life is sometimes easy; sometimes hard.

But there's always someone there to help you through it all.
One day it will get better, even without them with you.
Life takes the ones we love.
We will never get over them because we learn to accept,
But we will never forget.

Life shows us who we are,
Even if it takes all our strength.
God made life, us, and love.

Life is a blessing,

To the born and unborn.
Life is a great thing.
To the ones who need help through tough times, look up,
Remember who you care about...

..All the people who love and care about you!

Life is life.

Written By: Megan Smithers

The Little Boy in the Candy Cane Striped Onesie ~

The creaking chairs and the noise of soft whispers

silencing the chaotic mind of someone with a loss.

The mother of the bride-groom's soft, pained tears,

like dominoes, triggering a nuance of louder sobs

within the crowd. The father's light smile proves

him to be the most wounded of the rest, hiding his

sentiment. The feeling of a filched life; hugs for

the mother and the same old looks repeatedly

screaming, "I'm sorry" instead of "Thank you."

No charcoal or asphalt fabrics, rather, baby blues,

greens, and soft, soft pinks. The mother's instinct

of peace as he lies in the welcoming arms of the

Lord. "Sweet dreams, little Angel."

Written By: Kirsten Thieman

Perspectives ~

One might watch as…

Fresh emerald grass sways in the breeze;
Vibrant dandelions accrue under the
Sun's golden rays;
Small creatures encourage the lively foliage;
Cotton candy clouds suspend from azure skies;
And soaring birds adventure through
The ever-changing atmosphere.

But to another…

Desolate prairies remain still,
Offering a feeling of restlessness;
Weeds subjugate the surrounding plantation;
Insects aggravate the leaves of the harvest;
Thunderous clouds castigate the gazer's eyes;
And ignoble aviators seek the impassable.

Written By: Kirsten Thieman

My Love Language ~

I cannot tell you, I'm hurt,
But I can cry.
I cannot tell you, I'm sorry,
But I can hug.
I cannot tell you, it's going to be okay,
But I can smile.
I cannot tell you, I love you,
But I can kiss.

Written By: Tina Bryant
~ Autism Awareness

Stars ~

Have you ever sat outside in the night,
Looking up toward the sky,
Wondering what is behind,
Those beautiful stars?

Perhaps the greatest beauty,
Our eyes can't behold,
Is hidden behind the curtain of stars.

I believe God has angels,
Waiting for the Father to say,
"Open the curtain of the stars!"

I think he will let the world see,
What Jesus has prepared,
For you and me,
Behind those beautiful stars.

Now if you don't know Jesus,
You won't be blessed;
By the opening of the stars,
And the beauty behind them.

So now I tell you, this is the time,
To let Jesus into your heart.
Before God opens,
The curtain of the stars.

****For you my brightest stars,*
I love you always! Your friend, Mary Bryant

Dedications:

Faith Walks On Water pg. 75 – Dedicated to my friend Lindsey Brewer and her family ~ *One of Lindsey's paintings inspired this poem with title credit going to her father.*

Waterfront Romance pg. 95 – Dedicated to Tina Bryant with love

I Am My Brother's Keeper pg. 98 – Dedicated to my two brothers,

Craig Thieman and Curtis Thieman

In the Hands of Love pg. 99 – Dedicated to my wonderful parents,

Larry Thieman and Debbi Moore

Letters from Home pg. 100 – Dedicated to all who sacrificed their lives serving

A Grandfather's Legacy pg. 132 – Dedicated to the McRary family

Heart to Heart pg. 134 – Dedicated to the Hart Family

My Beautiful, Infant Son pg. 136 – Dedicated to all those who have experienced this type of loss.

A Christmas of Love pg. 142 – Dedicated to my dear friend Mary Bryant

A Star Is Born pg. 143 – Dedicated to Harley Laxton

101 Treasurable Poems of Faith, Hope, and Love

The following is a selection from the author's first 101 poetry collection.

~ Available at all major online bookstores.

A Lonely Vessel

Like a lonely vessel I sail alone; across this vast ocean, to and fro I roam. When there seems to be signs of life, I will send the lifeboats out; only to find nothing at all in the end, except for fear and doubt.

This ocean is but a graveyard, of those glorious ships of the past. Whatever happened to those ships, whatever happened? I dare to ask.

I looked forward to peace and tranquility, after the storm had finally passed; but now it seems to be me, by myself, with no other vessels left.

Still I voyage out, across that peaceful calm, with fervent expectation and hope; That one day, I'll see on the distant horizon, a line of sails from those grand ships arising!

Message in a Bottle

A message to my love I sent; a poem with the sweetest words. I told of the longing in my heart, and the love imprisoned there from the start. Then I rolled it up and placed it in a small glass bottle, empty within. I took the bottle with my message in there, down to the riverbank where time laid bare. I prayed this message, God would give her, and threw it in that lonely river. I thought, one day my love will find this bottle that I send, and upon opening it up, discover my love there within.

Sandcastles

Seeking success, I devise my own plan, building a castle with a foundation of sand. *I am a creator*, I say in my heart, then a wave comes and tears my castle apart.

Each time I tell myself, *this time it will last*; for many castles have fallen in the past. Yet, still each night that tide rolls in, and I have to begin building all over again.

My pride has blinded me from the truth, I think there's something that I need to prove. So I build a sandcastle again with my hands, and admire the masterpiece created by man.

Every night the tide washes it away, and I start all over again, on the very next day. Ignoring humility and God's loving plan, I keep building sandcastles here in the sand.

The Fisherman

An old man sat on a pier. In one hand, he held a fishing pole, as the other he moved about; while his stories were being told. This scene seemed quite silly, for many times, I did behold. This fisherman was my father. I thought him, crazy and old.

He told tales of a young, wise man, who once lived by the sea; a man my father called "Master," for a following of fishermen had he. Some people laughed at him, and claimed he had lost his mind; While others drew near to listen, at least from time to time.

One day he handed me a Bible, in brown paper tied with twine. If only I knew in that moment, it would be our last goodbye. Now I'm the old fisherman, found sitting on this pier; with that worn out fishing pole, I speak to all who will hear. Sure some people laugh at me, and claim I've lost my mind; But others will draw near to listen, at least from time to time.

Words Left Unspoken

They say you should tell her, the way that you
feel; they say you should let her know, what is
there in your heart. So maybe I am only a fool,
with his heart that is broken. I let you leave,
with words left unspoken.

I know it's probably too late, to let you know
now. For now we are separated, by so many
miles, but from my heart to your heart, consider
it a token; of how I feel about you, in these
words left unspoken.

*I have loved you from the beginning, from the
moment we first met. I remember your smile,
and I could never forget.*

When you left that one night, from that dream
I was awoken, because of those words, the ones
I left unspoken.

101 Treasurable Poems of Life, Love, and Light

The following is a selection from the author's second 101 poetry collection.

~ Available at all major online bookstores.

A Marvelous Waterfall

Your love has me in marvelous awe, your mercy is like a waterfall; pouring over me that I may find, renewing for this soul of mine.

Give me to drink, from this fountain each day. Let me dance in your mist and spray. Hands held high, reaching toward the sky; I will sing to you, and lift my voice in praise.

Your love is like a steady cascade, falling down from up on high. My sins are being washed away, a vessel filled that once was dry. I am drawn to this magical place, where your love and mercy flow; A waterfall of amazing grace, eternal life for this newly washed soul.

Beneath A Lover's Waterfall

Two lovers walking through the wood, on a hot summer's day; before reaching a small clearing, they felt the coolness of her spray.

Through brush and through grass, they had traveled the beaten path; down to the base of the falls, surrounded by eroded, rocky walls.

Leaving their things on the river's edge, they leaped off the small, stony ledge; into the foamy, sparkling pool below, beneath her mist and rainbow.

They swam across her open pool, halfway to the other side. Beneath the plunging waterfall, these two lovers took to hide.

They kissed and held one another, and then they laughed and played; beneath a lover's waterfall, on a hot summer's day.

When Rain Becomes Waterfalls

When rain becomes waterfalls, we find the joy in it all. Troubles no longer define us, no matter how big or small; When the rain that we experience, becomes a waterfall.

For in that moment; we realize, our suffering leads to great beauty, as the water fills the streams, filtered through the rocks of dreams; where raindrops gather one by one, and the water flows as one.

So when the rain in life begins, seek the Father, up in Heaven. Don't be afraid of what's ahead; don't harbor feelings of fear or dread. Remember in your suffering and pain, waterfalls are made from rain!

My Sandcastle Princess

Building a sandcastle, she looks up with a smile;
"Daddy, can you come, and play for a while?"
I told her I would, and to put her feet on mine;
And I danced in the sand, with that princess of mine.
My sandcastle princess, how the time has flown by;
Her wedding day is here, and she's starting to cry.
I wipe away her tears, not knowing what to say.
My sandcastle princess, is getting married today.
The years have passed by, and seasons have changed;
But time has a way, of healing the pain.
Building a sandcastle, she looks up with a smile;
"Grandpa, can you come, and play for a while?"
I told her I would, and to put her feet on mine;
And I danced in the sand, with that princess of mine.

The Christmas Rose

In the fields and the valleys, flowers come and go;
Through spring and summer, they bloom and grow.
Through wind and rain, they strive to remain,
But all have their time, when nature takes her toll;
They wither and die beneath the leaves and the snow,
All except one... The lovely Christmas Rose.
It may lay dormant at times, but again it will grow;
It can bloom in the winter, in the darkness and cold.
It blossoms within us, the young and the old;
All who believe, in the Christmas Rose.
It is planted within, a seed of faith and of hope;
Sown with great care, a flower so fair.
Within us it grows, when it will bloom;
Nobody knows, but the Father above,
Who planted with love, this lovely Christmas Rose.

Index

*** Bonus short stories (not included in the 101)

Knowing the LORD:

How is the believer really supposed to live? A believer is called to live a life of complete surrender. This means denying themselves and taking up the cross of Christ daily, to let him live through them. That is what a true believer looks like, and there are many out there who claim Christ when it is convenient, but they do not let Christ have control. They don't invite God's Spirit to enter in, possess, and change them. Now is the time for the people of Christ to ascend in Christ to that higher level of faith and living. Ask for the Father's Spirit, deny selfish personal desires, learn to love and forgive your enemies, and live life using your talents, gifts, and resources to manifest God's dream; for this is the pilgrimage and the personal ministry of those who are given over to the one and only true God, the Father.

Pray this:

~ Father please forgive me of all my sins. I am crucified with your Son, Jesus Christ. I partake in his baptism, and I give your Spirit full authority over this flesh of mine. Please come in and possess me Father, fill my heart, mind, and soul with your Spirit, and help me live like Christ.

If you truly believe what you prayed, then God is faithful to grant you His mercy and give you His Spirit. The next step is physical baptism among witnesses, getting involved with the people of Christ, and sharing the Gospel with others. I wish you only the greatest success in our Lord Jesus Christ!

~ Blessings Overflowing

In Conclusion:

~ I try to weave many mysteries of the Kingdom of God within my poetry, proverbs, and parables.

This anthology and trilogy was intended to be read in order. I believe these books can feed Christ's sheep, through proclaiming the fullness of the Gospel, to those who are called into the promise of Christ.

101 Treasurable Poems Series:

Faith, Hope, & Love - focuses on salvation, and God's Spirit flowing down upon us, filling us within.

Life, Love, & Light - focuses on enlightenment, and God's Spirit blooming deep within us.

Body, Soul, & Spirit - focuses on the greatest manifestation of Christ and his Kingdom, as the Spirit of God shines through us, a great beacon of light for others to follow in.

Challenge 1 – Write a coastal poem.

Challenge 2 – Write a romantic poem.

Challenge 3 – Write an inspirational short story.

May the peace and grace of

Our Lord Jesus Christ,

Be with you always!

Made in the USA
Middletown, DE
11 February 2017